GALÁPAGOS
Wild Portraits

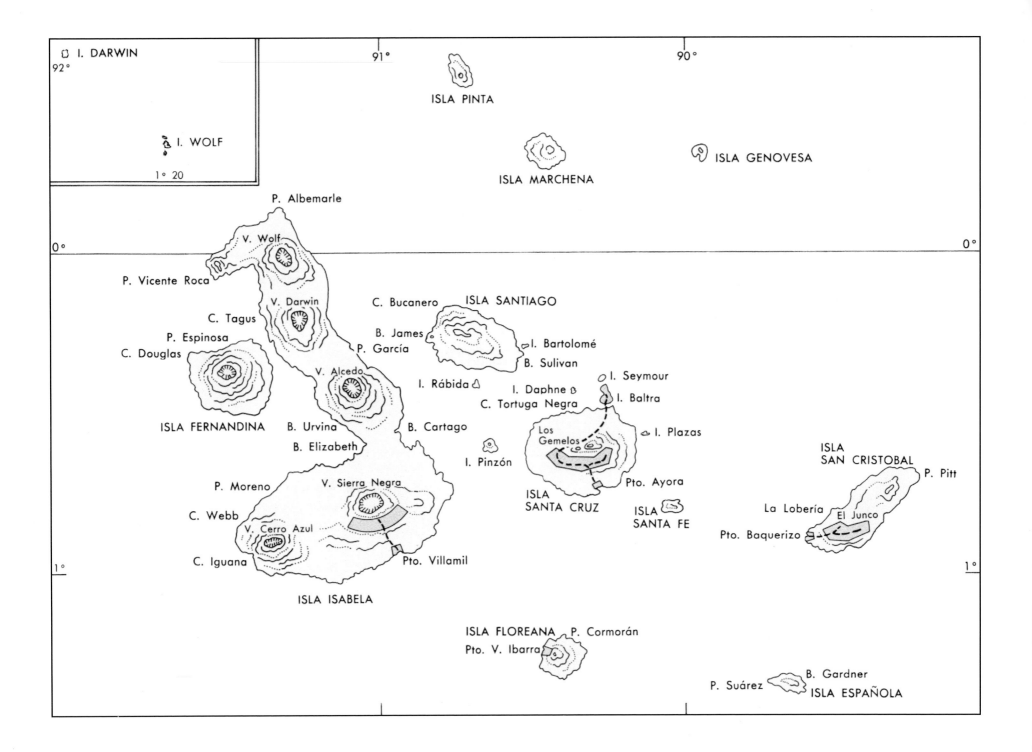

I. DARWIN
92°

I. WOLF
1° 20

ISLA PINTA

ISLA MARCHENA

ISLA GENOVESA

91°

90°

0°

0°

P. Albemarle

V. Wolf

P. Vicente Roca

V. Darwin

C. Tagus

P. Espinosa

C. Douglas

P. García

V. Alcedo

ISLA FERNANDINA

B. Urvina

B. Elizabeth

B. Cartago

C. Bucanero

ISLA SANTIAGO

B. James

I. Bartolomé

B. Sulivan

I. Seymour

I. Rábida

I. Daphne

I. Baltra

C. Tortuga Negra

Los
Gemelos

I. Pinzón

I. Plazas

ISLA
SAN CRISTOBAL

P. Moreno

V. Sierra Negra

P. Pitt

C. Webb

Pto. Ayora

V. Cerro Azul

ISLA
SANTA CRUZ

ISLA
SANTA FE

La Lobería

El Junco

C. Iguana

Pto. Villamil

Pto. Baquerizo

ISLA ISABELA

1°

1°

ISLA FLOREANA   P. Cormorán

Pto. V. Ibarra

B. Gardner

P. Suárez

ISLA ESPAÑOLA

GALÁPAGOS
Wild Portraits

Greetings,

Tui De Roy

Tui De Roy & Mark Jones

The Roving Tortoise
Worldwide Nature Photography

*This book is dedicated to
all who have learned how to love and respect
wildlife and wilderness.*

Concept and Design:
THE ROVING TORTOISE WORLDWIDE NATURE PHOTOGRAPHY
"Images from our planet's most pristine, uninhabited regions"

GALÁPAGOS - WILD PORTRAITS
is a completely new revised and redesigned version of
PORTRAITS OF GÁLAPAGOS, first published in 1990.
        Further editions 1991, 1993, 1995, 1997, 2000
        Spanish edition 1991.

Copyright © 2006 Tui De Roy & Mark Jones.

ISBN -10: ISBN-9978-45-035-1
ISBN -13: ISBN-978-9978-45-035-2

Endpapers:
Tui De Roy

Printed in Ecuador by:
IMPRENTA MARISCAL - Quito

About the Authors

Tui De Roy and Mark Jones are both originally from Europe. In 1955, Tui came to Galápagos from Belgium with her parents at the age of two, and was entirely home taught, gleaning much of her knowledge from her unique surroundings. Mark moved to the islands from England, where he was studying applied biology and environmental science, to work as a licensed naturalist and dive guide in 1981. Whether investigating an active volcano, observing courting penguins, or diving among whales and sharks, the peace and harmony of the natural world is their greatest source of happiness. Now internationally respected authors and photographers, their many years of Galápagos experience honed wilderness skills that have served them in their extensive travels through many of the world's most pristine, uninhabited regions. Their work has earned them numerous awards and commendations in North America, Europe and Asia. Publishing credits include hundreds of magazine feature articles in more than 25 countries, with almost a dozen book titles to their names, including translations into five languages. Nowadays based in New Zealand, though separated, they continue to work together under their partnership logo "The Roving Tortoise Worldwide Nature Photography". Operating on a freelance basis, they are as much at home climbing into the Amazon rainforest canopy to photograph a harpy eagle as camping amongst vicuña herds in the high Andes, or sailing in the Roaring Forties to remote Subantarctic islands aboard their custom outfitted expedition cutter, MAHALIA. Through their photography and writing, they dedicate themselves to converting their passion for the natural world into conservation action, and continue to spend a large proportion of their time working for the preservation and future of Galápagos. Tui sits on the Board of Directors of the prestigious Galápagos Charles Darwin Foundation, as well as the Boards of Advisors for the Galápagos Conservation Fund, Sea Shepherd International (for Galápagos) and the International Galápagos Tour Operators Association. Previously published books: GALÁPAGOS: Islands Lost In Time (1980), WILD ICE: Antarctic Journeys (1990), DAWN TO DUSK IN THE GALÁPAGOS (1991), PORTRAITS OF GALÁPAGOS (self-published, 6 editions), GALÁPAGOS: Islands Born Of Fire (1998), SPECTACULAR GALÁPAGOS (1999), GALÁPAGOS - Aus Feuer Geboren (German Language only, 2000), THE ANDES: As The Condor Flies (2005), NEW ZEALAND: A Natural World Revealed, (2006). They are currently working on ALBATROSS: Their World, Their Ways, and a guidebook THE NEW ZEALAND ROADSIDE WILDERNESS.

Signed copies of books can be mail-ordered — for price and shipping details contact:
<books@rovingtortoise.co.nz>

Introduction

For every Galápagos visitor, past or present, these islands evoke a very different vision. Whether regarded through horrid, life-threatening sagas, or described in tones romantic to the point of lyricism, one sentiment is shared by all: the utter power of their wildness engraves itself upon the human psyche, never to be erased. Whether this message is perceived as scars or as enrichment, a curse or a blessing, depends entirely upon the circumstance and state of mind of the observer.

When the Spanish Bishop Fray Tomás de Berlanga and his crew, near death from lack of water, first sighted the Galápagos Islands in 1535, they found only diabolical specters in a land on which it seemed "God had showered stones". Long before him, the Incas, on a mythical journey into the Pacific, had coined the foreboding name "Island of Fire". Nor did Charles Darwin see any beauty when he landed three centuries after Berlanga, although he was famously inspired by the archipelago's inimitable wildlife to formulate his revolutionary theory of evolution. To the buccaneers who plundered the coast of Spanish America in the seventeen hundreds these isolated volcanoes became a secret refuge where they could relax and rejoice safe from any reprisals. Yet in the eyes of Herman Melville, who later sailed here aboard a whaling ship, they once again become a hellish, if fascinating, location. Under the pen of contemporary writers, they alternate between a primal, undisturbed paradise where one can feel emotional kinship with the trusting animals, and the most desolate landscape of cinder, ash and mournful lava streams.

In this realm of stark simplicity, indescribable beauty and overwhelming magnetism our own personal destiny was cast through a complementary blend of intense interest, opportune coincidence and sheer chance. This fateful combination enabled us to explore a magical environment, absorb its compelling atmosphere and query the private lives of its wild denizens. It has never been clear to us whether our quest has followed the analytical considerations of the naturalist, the naïve curiosity of the child, or the simple consequential reality of each answer unavoidably raising an intriguing string of newer questions. This is of little relevance, for we are content in the knowledge of our ignorance. We do not pretend to understand the hammerhead shark any better than the tortoise understands the flycatcher that perches on his back. Nor do we have the right to. Their fleeting lives are both as unimportant and as vital to us as they are to each other, or as ours is to them. All we ask is to be allowed to witness the strands of life, large or small, rare or thriving, that are the very spirit of these outpost islands; to be a spectator to the trials and tribulations, the mundane and the tragic, that makes up each individual animal's day. And to this end, the rewards of Galápagos are boundless. Whether seeing a cormorant guard its young against a predacious hawk, a newborn sea lion nuzzle its mother for the first time, or a booby shade its young chicks from the blazing sun, one gets a sense of intimacy and, yes, kinship. We have followed the female land iguana who travels miles into the bowels of an active volcano to lay her eggs in a propitious patch of sun-warmed cinders; we have marveled at the perfection in the dance of the albatross pair, perhaps rehearsed over thirty seasons or more; and we've watched the orphaned baby fur seal breathe its last breath upon the unforgiving lava shore. Each time we are left with a sense not so much of understanding, but simply of wonder and admiration for the intricacies of these lives, and an immutable feeling of gratefulness that we have been allowed the closeness to share in such moments, albeit as uninvited guests.

With us we carry our cameras, not searching for any particular subject, not intending to render a specific aspect of graphic behavior, much less a scientific document. Instead, we attempt to capture those fleeting moments when life is most vibrant, to preserve them on film better than our limited memories could ever transmit, and to share those instants with others so that perhaps they too may be inspired to learn, respect and ultimately protect these precious islands and their unique wildlife.

In this book we have assembled a collection of such images, gathered over the years, some commonplace, others never to our knowledge repeated. In these portraits of its wildlife we hope to impart a feeling for the very essence of the Galápagos Islands.

The Animals

GALÁPAGOS SEA LION (*Zalophus wollebaecki*)..**p. 20**
The noisy colonies of this endearing marine mammal are a never-ending source of entertainment for the human observer. There are young pups exploring all that is new, rambunctious adolescents cavorting in the tide pools, mothers suckling their newborns and always the stern bark of the territorial beachmasters patrolling the shoreline. The endlessly inquisitive youngsters never tire of playing with any intriguing item, from marine iguanas to boat lines, to shells, sea urchins and starfish. Their games often include body surfing or even blowing bubbles in the face of snorkelers. For mature bulls life is much more serious, and rivalry can lead to violent battle when competing for breeding territories. From the plaintive cries of pups, to the calling of homecoming mothers or growling bulls, day or night the colonies are never silent.

BLUE-FOOTED BOOBY (*Sula nebouxii*)..**p. 26**
A most extraordinary and acrobatic diver, this abundant seabird hunts the rich coastal waters of Galápagos by plunging from great height and using its wings and powerful webbed feet to pursue fish underwater. The male is considerably smaller than the female and is particularly adept at inshore fishing where it can dive with full force into extremely shallow water. On land the remarkable color of this booby's feet become the center of attention during its complicated courtship display, mates dancing, skypointing and saluting to each other. A colony in full synchronized courtship can be an amazing sight, with the sounds of the vibrant activity heard from afar. While one or two chicks are normal, blue-foots may raise up to three, or occasionally four, young if food is plentiful.

RED-FOOTED BOOBY (*Sula sula*) ....**p. 36**
This is a bird of the open ocean, where it feeds on flying fish by skimming the waves. Only very rarely seen in the central part of the archipelago, it nests by the tens of thousands on some of the outlying islands, especially Genovesa, and on Darwin and Wolf in the very north. Unlike the other boobies, red-foots build twig nests in trees where they raise but a single chick. Nesting is year-round and, because of the long distances parents must travel to feed their young, chicks grow extremely slowly. In Galápagos most adults are buff colored, with only their blue beaks and red feet standing out from the grey-brown vegetation, but about five percent of the population are a delicate white. With the two types interbreeding freely, the reason for this difference is not known, and is contrary to red-foots found on other tropical islands.

NAZCA BOOBY (*Sula grantii*)..**p. 38**
This is the largest of all the boobies and is perhaps the whitest of all seabirds, glowing brilliantly in the tropical sun. Formerly called masked boobies, the Galápagos birds have been recently described as a separate species from their counterparts found throughout the tropics. They are heavy, powerful divers, frequently plunging vertically from a height of 60 meters or more. They feed on schooling fish in offshore waters, and are very often associated with feeding groups of dolphins. Aggressive and noisy, they breed in small colonies mainly on outlying islands. Their nests, like the blue-foot's, are on the ground, thinly lined with pebbles and twigs. Strangely, while two eggs are normally laid, the older, stronger chick almost invariably kills its sibling by repeatedly attacking it and driving it from the nest. Even when food is plentiful it is exceptional to find two large chicks together.

BROWN PELICAN (*Pelecanus occidentalis*)..**p. 42**
An unlikely looking fish-eater, this ancient bird has developed a unique method of feeding by using its great bill and pouch as a kind of large dip-net. Plunge diving into dense schools of small fish, it may engulf as much as ten liters of water, which it then strains out slowly to retain only the hapless fry. It also learns to associate with other species that might make fishing easier, such as sea

lions, penguins or boobies, and is not averse to handouts from people. As a result pelicans are frequently seen around boats and piers, where they sometimes get into trouble by getting caught on fishhooks. Around the ports they have learned to hunt at night on fish attracted to bright boat and jetty lights. They breed in small colonies in quiet, mangrove-fringed bays where up to 3 or 4 gangly chicks are raised in a large, loosely-woven twig nest.

These remarkable seabirds have mastered the art of aerial life better than any other bird on earth. Weighing only just over one kilo, with a wingspan of two meters, frigatebirds possess the greatest wing surface to body weight ratio of any bird. For endless hours they may soar high over the ocean without a single flap of the wings, effortlessly riding the slightest updraft. Indeed, there is no Galápagos sky that is devoid of their graceful black silhouettes. They can eat, drink, bathe, preen and perhaps even sleep on the wing. Two species, the greater and magnificent frigates, nest in various colonies around the archipelago. One of the largest is on Genovesa, where, between February and April each year, male greater frigates begin their fantastic courtship display by inflating an enormous red air balloon called a gular sac. The skin of the throat, which loses all of its color and size at other times, may be inflated or deflated at will in about 20 minutes. The resplendent males perch in low vegetation, fluttering their wings to appeal to females patrolling overhead. The life of the frigatebird is not an easy one, and it may take a pair nearly two years to raise their single chick to independence.

Like many seabirds this is another open ocean species that never comes to land except to nest. Because of its smaller size it chooses crevices and deep cavities in the face of sheer cliffs where it is safe from predators such as frigates and owls. The courtship flight, when small flocks come together, screaming loudly and circling on the sea wind, is one of the most beautiful Galápagos sights. Frigatebirds, always on the lookout for any feeding opportunity, often harass the unfortunate tropicbirds, even grabbing them by their streaming tail feathers, until they relinquish the fish they are carrying back to their nest. Like pelicans and boobies, tropicbirds feed by plunge-diving from the air in pursuit of their prey, although not usually so deep.

This unique cormorant has completely lost the use of its wings and is totally restricted to the shores of Isabela and Fernandina Islands. The largest species in the family, it is an excellent swimmer and feeds in the inshore shallows, carefully exploring the rocky bottom where it stalks eels, octopus, damselfish, scorpionfish and many others. Nesting only a few paces from the water's edge, cormorant pairs construct large nests from organisms brought back from the sea, such as seaweed, starfish, sea urchins and black coral, with individual nests often showing the particular preference of its owners. Courtship is also geared toward the sea, where couples perform a spiraling water-dance. Flightless cormorants are among the least numerous of Galápagos birds and could therefore be very susceptible to human impact.

This beautiful seabird is not only one of the most elegant birds of Galápagos, but it is also unique in the world. Unlike all other gulls it is completely nocturnal in its feeding habits, having developed huge eyes for night-vision, and white facial markings that enable the chicks to recognize their parents in total darkness. Nesting at all times of year in small colonies scattered over the archipelago, the gulls perform most of their courtship displays toward sunset and dawn. As night begins to fall a steady stream of the graceful birds can often be seen against the darkening sky, flying far out to sea to catch fish and squid. About 12,000 pairs nest along the edges of many Galápagos cliffs, but leave the archipelago altogether when not breeding, moving south to the cool waters of the Humboldt Current off Peru.

Along the coast hawks may take young seabirds, marine iguanas, or scavenge birthing sea lion placenta. Elsewhere they catch finches, lava lizards, snakes and insects, such as centipedes or grasshoppers. And where introduced goats run free they may even attack and kill the young kids. Though nests are rarely seen, their breeding habits are also remarkable, with a polyandric system in which up to three males may defend the territory and share parental duties with one female.

Whether in the green highlands of Santa Cruz Island or the dark lava fields of Genovesa Island, it is perhaps surprising, but not unusual, to spot an owl hunting in broad daylight. This adaptable species is actually nocturnal wherever the Galápagos hawk is found, but happily hunts in the daytime in the absence of hawks. Found on all the islands, they feed mainly on small birds and rodents in the interior, preying mostly on seabird chicks near the coast. On Genovesa owls can often be seen sitting quite still in the midst of the storm petrel nesting colony, their drab color blending perfectly with the lava, while they wait patiently for an inadvertent petrel to land within pouncing range.

In contrast to the dull colors of the abundant finches, the male vermillion flycatcher shines like a brilliant flower against the backdrop of greenery where it is most often seen. Rarely frequenting dry coastal regions, it normally lives in the misty highlands, perching and nesting in soft beds of epiphytic ferns and mosses that festoon the upland trees. While the pale yellow female tweets discreetly in the damp forest, the male frequently performs a dizzying territorial flight by slowly ascending high over the treetops, calling constantly and glowing in the sunlight, then plunging vertically back down to one of his favorite perches.

Every meter of dry lava coast or cactus scrub is owned and actively defended against others by one of these adaptable little reptiles. In all, seven species are endemic to Galápagos. Quick and sharp-eyed, they feed mainly on insects, from ants to large grasshoppers, scorpions and even the redoubtable large centipedes. However, they will also eat flowers and fruits, small crabs and sometimes scavenge carrion. They are clever at taking advantage of larger animals that might inadvertently provide an easy feeding opportunity, such as sleeping sea lions or basking marine iguanas, by perching boldly on their heads or bodies to snatch flies. Each male guards a territory where he allows several females to set up their own smaller plot, using rocks, logs or any high point to define the boundaries and survey their little domains.

These are quiet, solitary reptiles that make their living in the harsh dry interior of many of the islands, where they live in deep burrows dug in the volcanic soil or in natural lava caves. A typical land iguana's day begins slowly, emerging to bask in the morning sun, then setting off on the regular round of its territory in search of edible plants, and particularly fallen cactus fruits and pads which are often its only source of water. First it laboriously scratches and rolls these on the ground to remove as many of the spines as possible before swallowing great juicy mouthfuls. As the day heats up the iguana will return to the cool shelter of its burrow, emerging again in the afternoon. On many islands, land iguanas have special nesting grounds to which the females may migrate over long distances during the short periods of egg laying. One such area is inside the active caldera of Fernandina Volcano, in spite of the disastrous effect of periodic volcanic eruptions.

Almost no stretch of Galápagos shoreline, whether high vertical cliffs, barren lava fields, or busy town pier, is without its resident marine iguanas. No other lizard in the world has adapted to feed on seaweed. Indeed, it is an extraordinary sight to watch as each day at low tide the slender, dark reptiles move down over lava boulders to the water's edge where they cast themselves into the pounding surf. Most of the younger ones feed on exposed rocks, clinging with their sharp claws to resist the wave action, while larger individuals may swim some distance offshore and dive to the bottom to graze on the short algae with their specially adapted teeth. When they return they are exhausted by the cold water and must bask in the sun for many hours to regain their temperature, frequently "spitting" concentrated salt from the nasal glands that enable them to drink seawater. They have no need for shelter as they can control their heat intake by changing the orientation of their bodies to the sun. Highly sociable, they often lay comfortably in great tangled masses, although during the brief breeding period at the beginning of the warm season males do become aggressive, threatening each other with bobbing heads and sometimes engaging in energetic battles.

SALLY-LIGHTFOOT CRAB *(Grapsus grapsus)* ....*p. 84*

These brilliant red crabs, abundant on all the islands, add a striking splash of color to the black lava shorelines. They are fascinating to watch, scurrying about the rocks or over the backs of marine iguanas, "running" over the surface of quiet pools to evade predators lurking below, fighting or mating, yet continuously picking tiny morsels of seaweed as they walk. Avid scavengers of dead fish or meat wherever the opportunity arises, they also fall prey to a whole array of predators above and below water, such as herons large and small, octopus and moray eels.

GALÁPAGOS PENGUIN *(Spheniscus mendiculus)*..*p. 86*

This is the second smallest and most northerly of the 17 species of penguins in the world, even ranging slightly above the Equator. It does, however, favor the cooler waters of the archipelago where the rich upwelling of the Cromwell Current surges around the shores of Isabela and Fernandina Islands, with the notable exception of one small colony at Bartolomé Island. Penguins are not common and do not nest in large rookeries, but rather select deep caves and hollows in the lava shoreline to raise their young hidden from the hot sun. Adults spend most of their days hunting for small schooling fish in shallow waters, returning to land in the late afternoon, where their plaintive courtship braying can be heard near dusk and throughout the night.

GALÁPAGOS FUR SEAL *(Artcocephalus galapagoensis)*..*p. 89*

Compared to the ubiquitous sea lions, these are retreating animals, found exclusively along rugged shorelines where there are plenty of shady caverns and overhangs for them avoid the hot sun. Their strange bellows and screams can often be heard yet the animals remain unseen. Better adapted for cold than heat, in the warm season especially they also spend much time sleeping in the water with only their flippers held out to the sun like sails. Not very active on land, they swim large distances to feed far out at sea, seeking the productive areas of upwelling. Closely following the moon cycle, they may remain a week or more out of sight of land when the nights are darkest, feeding on squid and fish species that rise from the depths in the absence of light, and sleeping at the surface during the day. Their thick fur, composed of long guard hairs and dense under-wool, traps a layer of air that keeps them warm against the water's chill.

SHARKS AND RAYS ....*p. 92*

The richness of the Galápagos marine ecosystem, still relatively untouched by world standards, rewards divers with some of the most beautiful and exciting scenes to be found anywhere in the underwater world. Ocean giants such as manta rays and whale sharks are frequent visitors to the plankton-laden waters, and it is not unusual to see a school of shy, exquisitely graceful hammerhead sharks or a squadron-like formation of eagle rays circling along an undersea wall. Inshore, the quiet mangrove-fringed bays with their thriving marine communities represent a little world unto itslef. Here, the sight of a school of elegant golden rays gliding gently just below the surface, like many of the captivating views of marine life in Galápagos, is an experience that commands silent contemplation. Equally unique and diverse as the terrestrial ecosystems, the complex marine environment is, sadly, being put under more and more pressure from indiscriminate exploitation and serious threats from over-fishing. Thus could easily be lost a treasure that is only barely understood and appreciated.

Galápagos sea lion

23

Blue-footed booby

30

Red-footed booby

Nazca booby

Brown pelican

43

Frigatebird

Red-billed tropicbird

Flightless cormorant

Swallow-tailed gull

Waved albatross

64

Greater flamingo

Great blue heron

Darwin's finches

Galápagos hawk

Short-eared owl

Vermillon flycatcher

Lava lizard

Land iguana

Marine iguana

Sally-lightfoot crab

Galápagos penguin

Galápagos fur seal

Sharks & Rays

Sperm whale

Bottlenose dolphin

Green turtle

Giant tortoise

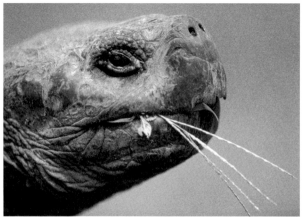

The Photographs

p. 1
A flightless cormorant dries its stubby wings at sunset, Fernandina Island.

p. 3
Giant tortoises wallow in a seasonal rain puddle, Alcedo Volcano, Isabela Island.

p. 4
Brown noddies snatch fish escaping a pelican's pouch, Santa Cruz Island.

p. 5
The endemic Galápagos dove inhabits arid islands, Española Island.

p. 6
A pair of waved albatross rest on a carpet of *Tribulus* flowers, Española Is.

p. 7
Two cows relax in the sun-warmed shallows, Fernandina Island.

p. 8
A Galápagos penguin shares a lava reef with sally-lightfoot crabs, Fernandina Island.

p. 9
Bottlenose dolphins frolic in clear waters, Roca Redonda, Isabela Island.

p. 10
Waves wash over a feeding marine iguana at low tide, Fernandina Island.

p. 12
A pair of blue-footed boobies courting on the beach, Seymour Island.

p. 13
Waved albatross pairs return to the same spot to nest each year in April, Española Island.

p. 20 left
A sea lion pup explores a black sand beach while mom is away feeding, Santiago Is.

p. 20 right
A young pup tries to find its mom amongst a group of cows, Fernandina Island.

p. 21
A group of adolescent pups cavort in the fine sand of Mosquera Island.

p. 22 left
A mother and her pup embrace asleep on the beach, Fernandina Island.

p. 22 top right
A cow gives birth in the late afternoon, Fernandina Island.

p. 22 middle right
A mother rolls over to suckle her newborn pup, Fernandina Island.

p. 22 bottom right
A young pup drinks rich milk from mother's retractable nipples, Fernandina Island.

p. 23 top
Bulls face off with loud barking where their territories meet, Mosquera Island.

p. 23 bottom left
Young bulls practice their strength by play-fighting, Genovesa Island.

p. 23 bottom right
A sea lion cow lounges in a tide pool, Fernandina Island.

p. 24 left
Ever playful pups loop round and round in a weightless world, Champion Island.

p. 24 top right
A cow glides effortlessly toward to surface for a breath of air, San Cristobal Island.

p. 24 bottom right
A sea lion dozes at the surface while fish school below, Sombrero Chino Island.

p. 25 right
Sea lions enjoy a speedy ride surfing inside a breaking wave, Seymour Island.

p. 25, sequence, top to bottom:
Bodysurfing sea lions leaping clear, within, and beneath the wave.

p. 26 left
A male blue-footed booby struts his stuff showing off his brilliant feet, Seymour Island.

p. 26 right
A pair of boobies dance in cadence to cement their nuptial bond, Seymour Island.

p. 27
Both male and female sway, whistle, honk and posture to impress each other, Española Island.

p. 28 top left
Deliberately stalling in a courtship landing, a male booby flashes his dazzling feet, Española.

p. 28 top right
A pair of boobies seem mesmerized by each other's colorful feet. Seymour Island.

p. 28 bottom
Blue-footed boobies rain onto a school of fish, hitting the water like arrows, Santiago Island.

p. 29
Loud whistles accompany the male's exaggerated landing display, Española Is.

p. 30, sequence:
Blue-footed boobies dance rhythmically, lifting their bright feet, bowing and skypointing.

p. 31
A skypointing male displays his acrobatic prowess to perfection, Española Island.

p. 32 left
A female (left) is larger, with darker eyes than her turquoise-webbed mate. Seymour Island.

p. 32 right
A male incubates by wrapping his warm webs around the eggs, Seymour Island.

p. 33 left
Until its down grows, a parent protects its young chick from the sun, Seymour Is.

p. 33 right
A well-fed chick is cared for by dedicated parents, Daphne Island.

p. 34-35, sequence:
Preening between parents and chick in a tender family scene, Española Island.

p. 36 left
Red-footed boobies courtship is more subtle than their blue-footed cousins, Wolf Island.

p. 36 right
The red-footed booby's face is even more beautiful than its bright feet, Genovesa Island.

p. 37 left
For reasons unknown, about one in 20 Galápagos red-foots is white, Genovesa Island.

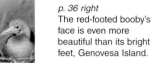

p. 37 right
A red-foot is busy building a nest in a shoreline red mangrove tree, Genovesa Island.

p. 38 left
A young Nazca booby stretches its wings to prepare for its first ever flight, Genovesa Island.

p. 38 top right
A fluffy Nazca booby chick appears larger than its parent, Genovesa Island.

p. 38 bottom right
An eager fledgling receives a meal from a parent freshly returned from fishing, Genovesa.

p. 39
A Nazca booby hangs on the wind before landing by its nest, Wolf Island.

p. 40
The Nazca booby was recently identified as a new Galápagos species of masked booby.

p. 41 top left
Boobies can look straight down their beaks to pinpoint fish, Genovesa Island.

p. 41 bottom left
Mates use their sharp beaks in gentle mutual preening, Genovesa Island.

p. 41 right
A Nazca booby pair, greeting at a sunset roost on Daphne Island.

p. 42
A brown pelican in breeding plumage bathes after fishing, Santa Cruz Island.

p. 43 top left
An adult brown pelican glides over calm inshore waters, Santa Cruz Island.

p. 43 bottom left
Pelicans are buoyant swimmers, Santa Cruz Island.

p. 43 right
A pelican in breeding colors rests on the shoreline after a day of fishing, Santa Cruz Is.

p. 44 top
A pelican dives for schooling fish in a mangrove inlet, Santa Cruz Island.

p. 44-45 five-shot sequence:
A diving pelican's pouch expands to entrap fish as its beak opens.

p. 45 top right
A diving pelican plunges down on a school of unsuspecting fish, Santa Cruz Island.

p. 46 top
A pair greets at the nest with open wings and swaying heads, Santa Cruz Island.

p. 46 bottom left
Hungry chicks dive into their parent's pouch for breakfast, Santa Cruz Island.

p. 46 bottom right
A pelican picks up a mangrove branch to build its nest, Santa Cruz Island.

p. 47 top
A parent returns from fishing to feed its fast-growing chicks, Santa Cruz Island.

p. 47 bottom left
Tiny hatchlings emerge from the eggs naked and helpless, Isabela Island.

p. 47 bottom right
In the first two weeks, the chicks white down and stubby beaks grow fast, Isabela Island.

p. 48 left
Magnificent frigatebirds hover expectantly when fishermen clean their catch, Santa Cruz Is.

p. 48 right
Two male frigatebirds compete in acrobatic flight over a nesting branch, Genovesa Is.

p. 49 top left
A female great frigatebird is courted eagerly by two males, Genovesa Is.

p. 49 bottom left
A courting great frigate male is inspected by two interested females, Genovesa Island.

p. 49 right
With his fully inflated pouch a male frigate performs a stunning display. Genovesa Is.

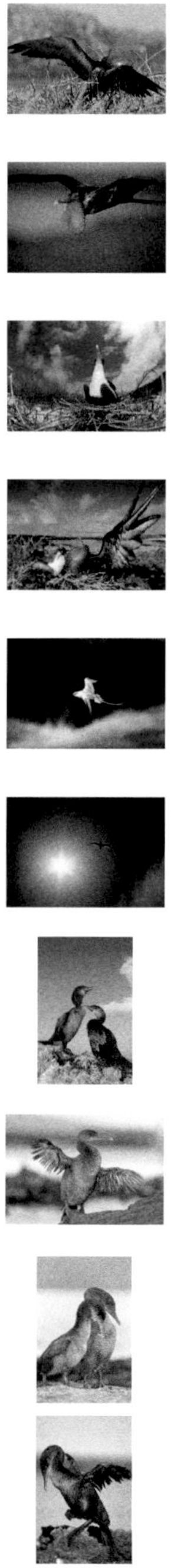

p. 50 top left
Two-meter wings outstretched, a great frigate male shimmers and dazzles, Genovesa.

p. 50 top right
Though he can deflate it if needed, a male flies with his pouch puffed up, Genovesa Island.

p. 50 bottom
A female great frigate incubates her single egg on her salt bush nest, Genovesa Island.

p. 51
Cooing and fluttering, a male puts on the full show to impress his mate, Genovesa Island.

p. 52
A red-billed tropicbird flies to its nest hidden in a deep cliff face fissure, Española Island.

p. 53
A tropicbird courts on the wing, approaching land only to nest, Genovesa Island.

p. 54 left
A flightless cormorant pair sits on their nest built of seaweed and starfish, Fernandina Is.

p. 54 right
After every fishing trip a cormorant must dry its waterlogged wings, Fernandina Island.

p. 55 left
Courting cormorants strut and hop along the lava shoreline, Fernandina Island.

p. 55 right
The cormorant's stunted wings are used only for balance, Fernandina Island.

p. 56
The world's largest cormorant, a nesting pair rests at sunset, Fernandina Island.

p. 57 left
A pair of cormorants' turquoise eyes contrasts with their drab plumage, Fernandina Island.

p. 57 right
A pair carefully places a pelican feather as a nest foundation, Fernandina Island.

p. 58 left
Swallow-tailed gulls mate at sunset, Genovesa Island.

p. 58 right
A swallow-tailed gull incubates its single mottled egg in a nest of pebbles, Genovesa Is.

p. 59 left
A tiny chick begs for a meal of squid from its attentive parent, Plazas Island.

p. 59 right
The nocturnal gulls head out at dusk to feed on squid far out at sea, Genovesa Island.

p. 60 left
The waved albatross is the only species living full time in the tropics, Española Island.

p. 60 right
A waved albatross rests amid *Sesuvium* plants tinted red in the dry season, Española Is.

p. 61
A waved albatross returns from feeding in rich but distant Peruvian waters, Española Is.

p. 62 top
Synchronized mutual gaping is part of the elaborate courtship, Española Island.

p. 62 bottom row
The complex courtship dance consists of a sequence of perfectly choreographed poses.

p. 63 left
A waved albatross uses a coral beach as a runway for take-off, Española Island.

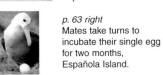

p. 63 right
Mates take turns to incubate their single egg for two months, Española Island.

p. 64 left
Amid seasonal flowers an albatross pair takes a break from courting rituals Española Island.

p. 64 right
A pair affirms its bond in a tender moment after a courtship session, Española Island.

p. 65
Snug in a plush down coat, a chick may wait days for a parental visit, Española Island.

p. 66 left
Greater flamingos engage in synchronized group courtship, Rabida Island.

p. 66 right
A flamingo's pink feathers are pigmented by the brine shrimp it feeds on, Rabida Island.

p. 67
A flock of flamingos wheel in unison over dry palo santo forest, Floreana Island.

p. 68 left
A great blue heron nesting in mangroves shields its eggs, Santa Cruz Island.

p. 68 right
Keen vision and dagger-like beak are good fishing tools, Santa Cruz Island.

p. 69 top
A successful stalk in a mangrove lagoon rewards a heron with a salema, Santa Cruz Is.

p. 69 bottom two
A hatchling marine iguana makes a quick meal, Fernandina Island.

p. 70 left
A vegetarian finch uses its cutting beak to peel unripe Croton fruit, Santa Cruz Island.

p. 70 top right
The largest of all beaks belongs to the large ground finch, Genovesa Island.

p. 70 bottom right
A cactus finch extracts Opuntia cactus seeds after piercing the fruit, Santa Fé Island.

p. 71 top row, left
A small tree finch gathers nesting material in the rainy season, Santa Cruz Island.

p. 71 top row, center
A large tree finch uses a parrot-like beak to feed on Solanum fruit in the Santa Cruz highlands.

p. 71 top row, right
A warbler finch picks insects in lush highland vegetation, Santa Cruz Island.

p. 71 middle row, left
A small ground finch is adept at feeding on a sedge stalk, Santa Cruz Island.

p. 71 middle row, center
A medium ground finch plucks green seeds from a spiny Scutia bush, Santa Cruz Is.

p. 71 middle row, right
A large ground finch cracks hard dry seeds fallen from Cordia bushes, Genovesa Is.

p. 71 bottom row
A woodpecker finch uses a cactus spine as tool to extract a fat wood-boring grub.

p. 71 right
A cactus finch uses its dagger-like beak to feed on an Opuntia cactus flower, Santa Cruz Is.

p. 72 left
A Galápagos hawk rides on the back of an unsuspecting giant tortoise, Isabela Island.

p. 72 right
Hovering on the breeze, a curious hawk inspects the visitor, Fernandina Island.

p. 73 left
A Galápagos hawk has no fear of people, approaching to investigate, Isabela Is.

p. 73 top
Master of his realm, a hawk flies over his territory, Isabela Island.

p. 73 bottom
A young iguana is a meal for a hawk, the top Galápagos predator, Fernandina Island.

p. 74 left
Hunting by day in the *Scalesia* forest, a short-eared owl takes a mouse, Santa Cruz Is.

p. 74 right
The brilliant male vermilion flycatcher is a highlands highlight, Santa Cruz Island.

p. 75 top
The male lava lizard is subtly marked with fine speckled designs, Santa Cruz Island.

p. 75 bottom
In contrast to males, the female lava lizard is brightly colored, Santa Cruz Island.

p. 76 top
A land iguana fattens up on lush rainy season vegetation, Isabela Island.

p. 76 bottom
In the dry season a land iguana finds moisture in a prickly *Opuntia* cactus fruit, Plazas Islands.

p. 77
Delicate *Portulaca* flowering after the rains provide sweet food for a land iguana, Plazas Is.

p. 78 left
Two marine iguanas bask together, Fernandina Island.

p. 78 right
A marine iguana rests on a sun-warmed boulder after feeding, Santa Cruz Island.

p. 79
Hundreds of marine iguanas pile up on the bare lava shore, Fernandina Island.

p. 80 left
To avoid overheating, these iguanas align their bodies to the sun, Fernandina Island.

p. 80 right
A young hatchling looks out for danger perched atop an impassive adult, Fernandina Island.

p. 81 left
Feeding in a shallow tide pool, an iguana comes up for air, Fernandina Island.

p. 81 top
An iguana swims along the surface by swaying its body, Fernandina Island.

p. 81 bottom
Iguanas escape a mosquito plague by sleeping in a tide pool, Española Island.

p. 82 left
Spray from a blowhole rains onto a young iguana feeding at low tide, Española Island.

p. 82 right
Anchored to the lava with sharp claws, an iguana lets waves crash over it, Santa Cruz Is.

p. 83 top
A brightly colored male Española marine iguana feeds in a tide pool near his breeding territory.

p. 83 bottom left
Seaweed growing in shallow water is the favorite marine iguana food, Española Island.

p. 83 bottom right
Legs trailing, an iguana swims toward the surface after grazing on the bottom, Española Is.

p. 84
Shunning the water, crabs join marine iguanas to evade the high tide, Mosquera Is.

p. 85 left
A sally-lightfoot crab is an easy meal for a lava heron hunting along the shore, Fernandina Is.

p. 85 right
Drab when young, adult sally-lightfoots exhibit many stunning colors, Santiago Island.

p. 86 left
A Galápagos penguin perches above sea urchins grazing the lava beds, Bartolomé Island.

p. 86 right
The Galápagos penguin is the only species at home in the tropics, Fernandina Island.

p. 87 top left
Resting on the lava shore, a penguin never ventures far from the water, Fernandina Is.

p. 87 bottom left
A small flock of Galápagos penguins set out to fish in the clear shallows, Bartolomé Is.

p. 87 right
Coming ashore in the afternoon, a penguin brays for a mate, Fernandina Island.

p. 88
Like a tiny torpedo, a penguin closes in on a school of fish, Sombrero Chino Island.

p. 89 left
To escape the heat a fur seal sleeps in the cool waters of a grotto, Santiago Island.

p. 89 right
Air trapped in the thick insulating coat of a fur seal escapes in fine bubbles, Cousins Rock.

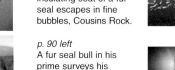
p. 90 left
A fur seal bull in his prime surveys his breeding territory, Fernandina Island.

p. 90 top right
A curious pup climbs on to a boulder to better investigate the visitor, Fernandina Island.

p. 90 bottom right
A fur seal pup mimics the restful pose of his mother, Fernandina Island.

p. 91 top left
A pup calls for his mother hoping she will soon return from fishing, Fernandina Island.

p. 91 bottom left
Friendly fur seal pups cavort together in a tide pool, Fernandina Island.

p. 91 right
A rambunctious pup climbs on his mother's back, Fernandina Island.

p. 92 top left
A school of golden rays gently circles in a peaceful mangrove inlet, Santa Cruz Island.

p. 92 bottom left
Spotted eagle rays glide over the white sand bottom of the bay in Santa Fé Island.

p. 92 right
A shy scalloped hammerhead provides a rare close encounter, Wolf Island.

p. 93
Hammerhead sharks mingle with constellations of creole fish, Wolf Island.

p. 94
Silhouetted by the sun's rays, a giant manta ray cruises the depths, Santa Cruz Island.

p. 95 top
Though rarely see, sperm whales frequent the rich, deep offshore waters.

p. 95 bottom
An undersea encounter with a mother and calf sperm whale can never be forgotten.

p. 96 left
Dolphins playing under the bows are one of the joys of Galápagos cruising.

p. 96 right
A bottlenose dolphin breaks the surface in a graceful arc off Roca Redonda.

p. 97
Playful bottlenose dolphins, at home in their underwater world.

p. 98 top
Common in Galápagos waters, green turtles drift weightlessly through the blue deep.

p. 98 bottom
A green turtle seeks out a quiet mangrove inlet to rest, Santa Cruz Island.

p. 98 right
A green turtle swims past an undersea wall, Cousins Rock.

p. 99 left
At daybreak a nesting female turtle covers her eggs before returning to the sea, Bartolomé Is.

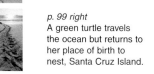
p. 99 right
A green turtle travels the ocean but returns to her place of birth to nest, Santa Cruz Island.

p. 100
The warm season, with clear morning skies and afternoon rains, elicits much activity on Alcedo.

p. 101
In the late afternoon, Alcedo's giant tortoises graze their way across rainy season meadows.

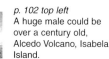
p. 102 top left
A huge male could be over a century old, Alcedo Volcano, Isabela Island.

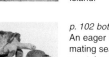
p. 102 bottom sequence
An eager male in the mating season overtakes his quarry.

p. 102 right
Like everything tortoises do, mating is a slow, ponderous affair, Alcedo Volcano, Isabela Is.

p. 103
As rain clouds gather, a tortoise heads for its favorite wallow on Alcedo Volcano.

p. 104 left
Taking advantage of the brief rains, tortoises flock to temporary wallowing pools.

p. 104 top right
A giant walks along the rim of the volcano at sunrise, Alcedo, Isabela Island.

p. 104 bottom right
No one knows why tortoises like to wallow, but getting rid of ticks could be a reason.

p. 105 top right
Following a well-worn path along the caldera floor, a tortoise carries a hawk as a rider.

p. 105 left
This tortoise greets the morning with a big yawn, Alcedo Volcano, Isabela Island.

p. 105 bottom center
When rains green the land, tortoises feed generously and replenish their energy.

p. 105 bottom right
Perhaps already a teenager, a young tortoise grows slowly, Isabela Island.

p. 106 left
Morning mist shrouds a tortoise pond, Alcedo Volcano, Isabela Island.

p. 106 top right
When the rains hit, a tortoise hurries toward seasonal pools.

p. 106 bottom right
Rain pummels the surface of a pond, Alcedo Volcano, Isabela Island.

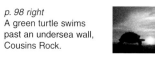
p. 107
The sun rises over a quintessential Galápagos scene, Alcedo Volcano.

p. 112
Parting shot: giant tortoises set out on their daily errands.

Acknowledgments

During the course of more than 30 years of Galápagos photography the list of people we would like to thank would inevitably fill many pages. There are those who helped us learn and discover, and who made many a precious experience possible. Scientists shared their knowledge and their expeditions. Park wardens welcomed us into their camps and took us on long, challenging field missions. Fishermen showed us secret anchorages and tour boat owners either invited us as their guests, or allowed us time to photograph while in their employ. Even if we can't thank them all here by name, each and every one is deeply appreciated — the memories of those shared moments are indelibly entwined with those of the wildlife itself. But there are also many more who not only helped us understand, enjoy and appreciate the Galápagos we so love to photograph, but whose entire lives are centered on fighting for their safe future. It is thanks to their efforts that Galápagos remains the place that it is today. For this we are forever grateful. Since the simultaneous inception of the Galápagos National Park and the Charles Darwin Foundation 45 years ago, both institutions have been staffed by a long succession of ardent conservationists whose energy has far, far exceeded any call of duty. Likewise, within the tourism industry some individuals have engaged the passion of the world in support of these precious islands, while in the meantime born and bred Galapagueños, espousing the changing times, are taking conservation leadership into their own hands. Most admirable of them all are those special few whose inner fires has steadfastly transcended both private life and professional opportunity. For their collective vision and tireless work, our deepest appreciation goes (in no particular order) to people like Miguel Cifuentes, Alan Moore, Jacinto Gordillo, Godfrey Merlen, Julian Fitter, Linda Cayot, Felipe Cruz, Karl Campbell, Washignton Tapia, Victor Carrion, Sixto Naranjo, Hernan Vargas, Manfred Altamirano, Roslyn Cameron, Craig MacFarland, Padraig Whelan, Howard and Heidi Snell, Alan Tye, Scott Henderson, Günther Reck, Eliecer Cruz, Rob Bensted-Smith, Sylvia Harcourt-Carrasco, Alfredo Carrasco, Maria Elena Guerra, Peter Kramer, Graham Watkins, Sven Lindblad, Lynn Fowler, Cindy Manning, Emma Ridley, Paula Tagle, Luis Verdesoto, Hans Schiess, Josefina Arevalo, and many, many more. By celebrating the untamed spirit of the wildlife on these pages, we wish to express our eternal gratitude to all of you for being the true guardians of Galápagos — and also for being our friends. And to our parents, our heartfelt thanks for supporting and understanding the paths we have chosen, and for your subtle guidance throughout life.